PROTECTION

SPELLS & CHARMS

BY JADE

ORIGINAL PUBLICATIONS
PLAINVIEW, NEW YORK

ORIGINAL PUBLICATIONS
22 East Mall
Plainview, New York 11803

ISBN: 0 - 942272- 48 - X

This Book is Dedicated to
the Memory of Scott Cunningham

To our friend and fellow author. We miss you greatly, but we do have
our memories of the great times we had together. Like the times at
Harvest Moon Festivals at Pierce College where we would talk about
and exchange information for our books we were writing. The 5:00
Friday night phone calls to the shop where we talked about every-
thing under the sun, our book signing, lectures at the shop and the
long talks and dinners together.
Scott, those great times will always be in our memories. Thank you
for them. We miss you, with love and deepest respect we dedicate
this book to you, our friend, Scott Cunningham.

Judith Defrain and Carey Vosburn
(JADE)

Table of Contents

Table of Contents

To Protect from Thieves in a Home

This spell must be done on a New Moon Night.

1. On a window in a mixture of **Protection Oil, Sun Oil** and **Four Thieves Vinegar** write the following:

> Darkness Lies...Where it is Born
> But Sunlight Flies...To Light this Room

2. Over a door in **King Solomon Oil** write:

> Who comes to me I keep
> Who goes from me I free
> Yet against all I stand
> who carry not my key

3. Burn **Protection From Thieves Incense** *(see recipe below)* each **New Moon** near the front and back doors.

1/2 Cup Sandlewood	1/2 Cup Myrrh
1/3 Cup Vetivert	1 1/2 Cup Lavender
1/4 Cup Cinnamon	1/4 Cup Cloves

4. Sprinkle **Protection from Thieves Powder** on all window sills once a month.

To Be Put in a Book to Loan Out

On the first page of the Book that you are lending out write in Dragon's Blood Ink:

For them that stealeth or borroweth and returneth not
this book from its owner let the book change
into a serpent in their hand and sting him.
Let book worms gnaw their entrails
in token of the worm that dieth not
and when at last they meet their end
let the flame of Hades consume them forever and aye.

Also rub some **Lavender Flowers** on your **Book** to ensure it's return.

To Protect Your Car From Thieves

1. Take a little **Oil** from the **Dipstick** and add some **Blessed Salt** and **Protection Oil.**
2. Anoint **steering wheel** and each tire with the mixture and say:

I say these words my spell to wind and
this spell this car I bind. So he who steals it through far away
will have no peace by night nor day.

Do this every 6 months on a New Moon Night.

To Protect Your Car From Accidents

1. Place **2 Claws** and some **Whiskers** from a **Cat.** Mix with some **Blessed Salt** and place in a **Red Flannel Bag** along with this **Talisman.**

2. Hang it over the **Dash** and say:

As these artifacts guided the beast they served
so let them guide this car (name it) thru danger
Give the car a name and call it by this name from now on
For example, "Good Morning Monty", when entering in the car
in the morning.

A simple working falsehood is more useful
than a non-functional complex truth.

Rose of Jerico Protection

1. On a **Full Moon Night** in a **Sun Hour,** take a **Bowl of Water** and stir the Water **clockwise.**

2. As the Water runs, drop in **3 Grains of Blessed Salt** in the bowl.

3. Anoint yourself with **New Life Oil** and place a plant in the bowl of Water at **9:00 am on Tuesday** or **Friday** and leave for 3 days or until **Green.**

4. At **9:00** each morning dip your **Fingers** of both Hands in the Water and say:

> Divine Rose of Jerico for the blessing
> received for the virtues that you hold and
> the power considered, help me solve
> the difficulties of life. Give me health, strength,
> comfort, and peace in my home.
> Bring luck to my business, ability in my work,
> bestow upon me the necessities for my home and family
> All this I ask for the virtues you hold in true an love

5. Replenish water as needed, and it will flourish forever.

6. Burn **Harmony Incense** in the home at least once a day.

To Protect Yourself From a Hex

On a Full Moon Night Blend:

1 Pinch of Thyme	7 Tsp. Basil
7 Tsp Sage	1 Pinch Salt Peter
7 Tsp. Garlic Powder	7 Tsp. Parsley Leaves
7 Drops Rose Geranium Oil	

1. Blend mixture well in a **Wooden Bowl** on a **Tuesday.**
2. Put a portion of the mixture in a **Mojo Bag** anointed with **Jinx Removing Oil** and carry with you.
3. Take a bath in the same mixture while burning a **Reversing Candle** and some **Jinx Removing Incense.**
4. Burn **Jinx Removing Incense** Daily in the Home.

This procedure will uncross any **Hexed Person** and will protect from being Hexed for 7 weeks. The procedure may be repeated.

5

Incantation Against Dangerous Individuals

Start this spell in a Saturn Hour on a Saturday

1. Put a **Lucky Hand Root** and a **Galangal Root** in a small bag.
2. Anoint with **Commanding Oil** and place on your altar between a **Red Candle** and a **Black Candle**. Burn **Set Incense** and say:

Come to me O' Lords of Gods,
Drive a far from me the Lions coming from the earth,
The crocodiles issuing from the river,
the mouth of all biting Reptiles coming out of their holes
Stop Crocodile Mako Son of Set
Do not wave thy tail
Do not work thy two arms
Do not open thy mouth
May the waters become as a burning fire before thee
The spear of the 77 gods on thine eyes
The arm of the 77 gods is on thine eyes
Thou who wast fastened with metal claws to the
bark of RA. Stop Crocodile Mako Son of Set
let the flame of Hades consume them forever and aye.

3. Write out the incantation on a piece of **Tin Foil**. Roll or fold up and place it in the bag with **Roots** and carry. Replenish bag each week by anointing with **Commanding Oil**.

After 9 months, burn bag and repeat procedure

To Control Troublesome Neighbors

1. Take **Hot Foot Powder** and **Controlling Powder** and sprinkle in a place where your neighbor will walk and they will stop bothering you.

2. Sprinkle **Peace Powder** in every corner to keep things peaceful.

3. Sprinkle **Jalap Powder** on the front steps. In the morning sweep it away. Continue this until all problems with your neighbors stops.

Treat everyone with kindness

Invisibility Spell

To be hidden from creditors, the law or anyone who might seek you to cause you harm.

1. Do this spell on a **Sunday** in a **Saturn Hour**. On a backside of a **Sixth Pentacle of the Sun**, write your name in **Dragon's Blood Ink** 3 times.
2. On a **Gray Candle** scratch names or titles of those you wish to be hidden from.
3. Anoint the **Candle** with **Saturn Oil** and burn **Saturn Incense** while concentrating on the Candle.
4. Place the **Candle** on top of the **Seal** with name on the bottom. Burn the **Candle** until it is consumes.
5. Take the **Wax** residue and **Seal** and place in a Cup or **Chalice** Cover with a **Gray Cloth**. Hide the **Chalice** away in a closet and never let Sunlight touch it.

Make yourself a bag with these items and carry with you.

Onyx	Bloodstone	Tigers Eye
Opal	Topaz	Chicory
Malefern	Heliotrope	Mistletoe
Poppy Flowers	Wolfsbane	

You will remain invisible to those you choose until you uncover the Chalice or it is disturbed!

To Banish a Ghost

1. Use **Broom Tops** (herb) boiled with **Salt** and **Rosemary**.

2. Strain and sprinkle in all the rooms, ending at the **Front Door** where you will hang a **Red Bag** full of **Spurge Seeds** to stop all **Poltergeist** activity.

3. Say this in a loud voice as you sprinkle the **Herb Brew:**

> I Banish Evil from this house all Ghost, Poltergeist
> and unseen evil be they Spirit, Fiend or Demon.
> Be banished and remove and return to the
> realms of the spirits. I command this by the power of the
> Archangel Michael and His Flaming Sword

To Discourage Unwanted Visitors

1. Soak a piece of **Parchment** paper in **Four Thieves Vinegar.**

2. When dry, write in **Dove's Blood Ink** the names of those people you do not wish to visit you.

3. Take the **Parchment** and wrap it around a **Broom Handle.** Use the Boom to sweep **Cowslip Flowers** under the Door Mat. The Broom is then places behind the door.

House Exorcism and Blessing

Prepare the Following:

Mojo Bags:

1. FRONT DOOR(S): Red Flannel Bag(s) with **Angelica Root** in them (to rid negativity) anointed liberally with **Protection Oil.**

2. BACK DOOR(S): Red Flannel Bag(s) with **Wormwood herb,** anointed liberally with **Uncrossing Oil.**

3. WINDOWS: 1 **Bloodroot** for each Window (for psychic protection) or a **Bethroot** (Low John) for each window for physical protection.

4. Set up a small portable altar table in the center of the first room. Make sure that the altar has:
   2 White Altar Candles.
   1 larger White Candle anointed with Protection Oil
   Blessed Salt
   Charcoal and Incense
   Uncrossing and Protection Oils
   Bell, Chalice of Water and an Athame

5. Your first room should be on the top floor for a 2 story house working down to the bottom floor and out the back door.

6. For a 1 story house with no back door, start at the back of the house and chase the negativity out the front door.

7. Light the altar candles and the incense in the first room. You will then concentrate with the salt and water by putting a little **Blessed Salt** in your water container and proceed to walk counter clockwise around the room, sprinkling the **Blessed Water** as you go. Be sure to include all closets, cupboards and drawers (attics and basements if the house has them).

8. Then take your largest **White Candle** and again walk around the room counter clockwise. When you are done replace the candle on the altar.

10

9. Next pick up your incense burner and repeat the process around the room and place the incense back on the altar.

10. Now take the bell and go to each direction (N, W, S, & E) in the room and ring the bell 3 times and call the name of the **Angel** of that direction 3 times.

11. When you are finished place the bell back on the altar and snuff (do not blow) out the altar candles and move to the next room, re-light the altar candles and start again.

North:	**Angel...Auriel**
West:	**Angel...Gadriel**
South:	**Angel...Mikiel**
East:	**Angel...Raphael**

12. Place appropriate **Mojos Bags** at doors and windows, with **Banishing Earth Pentagram** drawn in chalk or Oil over every door, opening window and mirror (every portal).

13. "Sweep" out all bag energy out a back/front door by chanting the **Shiva Chant** (Book of Hywww) let the incense and the candles burn out at the back/front door.

CHANT:

Lovely powerful Shiva, God of Sweeping change
Sweep away the lesser, shut it out of range
Leave the beauty and the light bright
clean and fair, remove all vibrations of misery and despair
leave this place, and these find things fresh
and bright and pure holy as your own fine self
bright complete and sure, lovely powerful Shiva
Our thanks to you we give, that from your sweeping power
in beauty may we live

This spell is especially helpful when moving into a new home!

F or Protection from Enemies and to Prevent from Being Hexed

1. Take some **Ague Weed**, burn on **Instant lighting charcoal** with **Evohe Incense** to destroy your enemies' power to harm you.

2. Place **Bay Leaves** in each corner of the house. Hang a bag of **Angelica** over the door while saying:

> **Spirits of the Light, will I see**
> **Spirits of the Light come to me**

A bloodroot placed on each window sill prevents further hexes.

T o Destroy Problems

Do this spell on a Sunday in a Sun Hour.

1. Burn a **Black Candle** in a bowl of **Knotweed**, **Jinx Removing Bath Salts** and **Honeysuckle Flowers**.

2. When Candle is completely burned, take the **Wax** and **Herbs** and **bury** them far from home.

3. Soak **Lions Tail herb** in a jar of **Salt** and **Water** in a sunny window for 6 days. On the **7th day** sprinkle the water around your home for luck.

To Force and Enemy to Move Away

1. On a **Full Moon** burn a **Reversing Image Candle** anointed with **Moving Oil** in a bowl of **Poke Root.** and **Get Away Powder.**

2. When the Candle has finished burning, take the wax and herbs and wrap them in a **Black Cloth** and throw into moving water.

A Protection Bag for Children

To protect a **Child** when they are out of your sight or during sleep, put the following **Herbs** and **Items** in a **White Bag** and sew it into a **Child's Pillow.**

Primrose	Sea Salt	Motherwort
Sea Shell	Rose Quartz	Woodruff
A Lot Love		

This is to insure respect, loyalty and safety of the Child

Protection at Night in Sleep

1. On a **Saturday** in a **Saturn Hour**, make a cloth pillow small enough to slip between pillow and pillowcase. Fill with these things:

   Mint - To Keep Evil Away
   Mistletoe - To Protect from Evil Spells
   Monkshood - To Repel Evil Spirits
   Oak Moss - To Attract Good Spirits of Protection
   Mugwort - For Pleasant Dreams
   Rosemary - For Blessing
   5 Finger Grass - For Protection from all harm the hand can do

Say this chant before going to sleep at night:

> Keep me safe all night long
> While Lightening rolls and Thunder flash
> Hold me calm, guard me strong
> while Lightening flash and Thunder rolls
> Secure from light till evensong

Before retiring at night, sprinkle a little **Fiery Wall of Protection Powder** on doorstep and say:

> Begone Evil, away with thee
> Darken my abode no more,
> Enter light
> you are welcome here
> Come in quick and close the door

To Stop Gossip

1. Chew a piece of **Chewing John (Galangal)** and spit in front of the house of those who spoke meanly to you.
2. In your home burn **Sandlewood Incense** and then stand in the center of the room facing the door. Evil thoughts and Evil Spirits will leave your house just as the fumes of the incense are vanishing. Do this for 9 days without fail.
3. Pour **1 tsp of Jinx Removing Bath Salts** in your bath water each night and burn **Helping Hand Incense** each morning and all scandal and gossip will stop.

Protection from Harm

1. Burn a **Black to White Candle** anointed with **Devil Trap Oil**.
2. Rub the **Oil** onto the door knob of your front door. Burn **Run Devil Run Incense** and say:

> Stretch forth they hands and protect me from
> undesirable harassments of this life
> Cause aggressors against me to become
> powerless to harm and unable to injury or
> destroy and incapable of inflicting damage on those
> whom I love and those that dwell herein.

To Uncross a House and Find Harmony and Happiness

1. On a **Sunday** in a **Sun Hour,** take a **King Solomon Root** and place it in a glass of water with **3 drops of Lavender Oil.**

2. Keep it in a **Sunny Window** for 3 days. On the **4th day,** sprinkle the water in every corner of the house.

3. Burn **John the Conqueror** and **King Solomon Incense** everyday in the morning.

4. Once a month wash the floors with **Van Van Floor**

5. Take a bath with some **Van Van Bath Salts.**

6. Anoint yourself with **Harmony Oil** before beginning your day and burn a **Pink and Blue Combination Candle** anointed with **Harmony Oil** for a few minutes while concentrating on happiness. Then snuff the candle out before going to sleep each night.

   Until the candle is completely burned, do not blow out the candle, snuff it out and relight the next evening and so on until candle is gone.

To Change a Bad Situation to your Advantage

Set your altar up as shown:

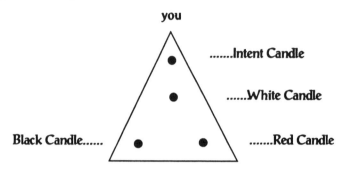

you

.......Intent Candle

.......White Candle

Black Candle......   ....Red Candle

1. Draw a triangle on the altar cloth in chalk and set the candles inside of the triangle as shown.

2. Write on the **Red Candle** Anger, *Hatred and Envy.* Anoint it with **Mars Oil.**

3. Write on the **Black Candle** whatever the problem is (for example *Evil Thoughts, Gossip,* etc.). Anoint it with **Pluto Oil.**

4. Write on the **White Candle** *Change and Be Transformed.* Anoint it with **Moon Oil.**

5. The **Intent Candle** may be whatever color suits your purpose. For example if you wish to change the negativity energy into MONEY for your benefit, use a **Green Candle** with **Money Draw Oil** on it. For SUCCESS use a **Yellow Candle** and **Success Oil.**

6. Light the **Black Candle** first and concentrate on gathering all negativity from around you and pushing it into the candle.
Then light the **Red Candle** and concentrate on gathering Anger and Hatred into it.

When you have a accomplished this, light the **White Candle** and imagine all the negativity and hatred transformed thru the **White Candle** into positive clean white energy pulsating and ready to be aimed at your intent.

7. Light your **Intent Candle** and visualize what you want. When you have concentrated for as long as you can, blow out the **Black and Red Candles** and snuff out the **White** and **Intent Candle.**

8. Repeat procedure daily until all candles have burned.

9. Burn **Moon Incense** while candles are burning and say:

Take from me any intention of harm and
turn away all destructive designs.
Transform them with truth and goodness.
Bestow in me wisdom and strength of character
and confidence so that I may attract abundant blessing

 ragon's Blood Spell

To Remove a Spell someone has placed upon you.

1 Take a Bath in **Jinx Removing Salt** and **Dragon's Blood Salt**.

2. Anoint yourself after the bath with **Dragon's Blood Oil.**

3. Write on 9 small pieces of **Parchment Paper** in **Dragon's Blood Ink** these **Rune symbols:**

4. In the center of each piece of **Parchment Paper** put a teaspoon of **Dragon's Blood Incense.** Fold the Paper up so Incense stays in place and anoint with **Dragon's Blood Oil.**

5. Anoint a **Red and Black Candle** with **Dragon's Blood Oil** and burn one package of the **Incense** and **Runes** on the Charcoal and say:

Those who have made images of me
Reproducing my features and using my artifacts
And who have taken away my livelihood
Harmed my relationships and chosen to do me harm

May the Fire Breathing Dragon, the Almighty Dragon
Break their charm

Blow out the candles and repeat the procedure the next 9 nights until all packages of runes and incense have been consumed.

When Life Has Failed You

1. To remove a condition, whether self imposed or inflicted by another, you need a **Black Candle** and **12 Straight Pins**.

2. Stick the pins in various positions until all the pins are used.

3. Pour **Saturn Oil** on the **Candle** and burn the Candle in a Bowl of **Goofer Dust** and **Asafoetida**.

4. Burn an **Incense Mixture** of **Agrimony, Mars Incense, Star Anise** and **John the Conqueror Incense** and say over the Candle as it burns:

Burn Incense
Burn consume this curse
and turn the evil back
Remove and defeat the lack
Burn, Candle burn
Turn Candle turn
Remove the spears
consume the fears

5. As the **Candle** burns the pins will fall, and the **Wax** will mix with powders. When all the Candle has burned, take all the **Wax, Pins** and **Powder** and place in a plastic bag. Throw the bag in the ocean or burn far from your home

To Return Evil to Sender(s)

1. If you know for certain who has placed a spell upon you and you wish to return the favor, draw a figure of the person on a piece of **Parchment Paper** in **Dragon's Blood Ink** or **Ritual Black Ink**.

2. Write their name(s) on it and when the ink is dry, rub the paper with a mixture of **Angelica** and **Agrimony Herbs** and **Camphor Gum**.

3. Each day you will light some **Elemental Incense** and tear off a piece of the **Paper Doll** and burn it in the **Incense** as you say:

Arise O Domballah!
O Victim you are seized, you are seized,
you are changed, your hands become stilled,
you legs bend, your back hunches, your neck twists,
you teeth fall out and your loins fester.
O Victim release your sufferer or you the martyr will be!

In 5-15 days the person will have moved,
disappeared or left you alone.

CAUTION:
Karmic damage may occur as a result of using this spell

To Treat Someone Who is Possessed

1. Mix:. **Queen of the Meadow**   **Balm of Gilead**
   Black Cohash   **Sulphur**

2. Burn this mixture at midnight outside the backdoor.

3. Mix: **Blessed Salt**   **Agar Agar**   **Wahoo Bark**
   Anise Hyssop

4. Boil mixture in **1 Qt. of Water** for 10 minutes and strain.
   Use tea to sponge the possessed and say:

> Be ye gone evil spirits,
> Be ye gone wicked demon - Be gone
> Be ye a wicked god - Be gone
> Be ye an evil phantom - Be gone
> Be ye an evil specter - Be gone
> Be ye an evil energy vampire - Be gone
> Be ye a succubus - Be gone
> Be gone, be gone, I command you in
> The names of
> Lo-Faham
> I-You-El
> I-OSen-We

** Now place upon the person a **Hexagram of Solomon Talisman**
that has been blessed by yourself.

To Protect Your Purse or Wallet from Being Stolen

On a Saturday in a Sun Hour, make a Mojo Bag containing these items:

Apache Tear	Quartz	Gentian Root	Garlic
Hyssop	Bittersweet	Luck Hand	Tiger's Eye Stone

Seal of the Sixth Pentacle of the Sun

Tie bag shut with 8 knots. Keep well rubbed with Protection from Thieves Powder or Protection from Thieves Oil or Protection from Thieves Vinegar once a month and carry in pocket or purse.

Banish Illness

Burn a **Black Candle** anointed with **Banishing Oil** and **Burn Banishing Incense.** Concentrate on removing whatever the health problem may be by saying:

> As this candle burns,
> So the illness turns,
> Melted like this wax,
> Cut like with an ax
> Remove and banished
> All disabilities vanished
> As my word you see
> Radiant health blessed be.

Let the candle burn until done. Then bury ashes from incense and any leftover wax.

⚕⚕⚕

Make the person a **Health Doll** by filling a **Yellow Doll** with an artifact of theirs, plus **Speedwell, All heal, Self Heal, Chamomile** and **California Poppy.**

Sew the Doll shut with **Yellow Thread.** Rub the Doll well with **Sun Oil** and make a gift of it to the ill person. They should sleep with it under their pillow.

Protection in a Psychic Attack

1. Take **4 Candles** - **2 Red** and **2 White**. Anoint with **Psychic Power Oil**.

2. Place in the 4 quantrants - **Red in North and South, White** - in **East and West**.

3. In the center of your **Altar** place a **Cauldron** with **Charcoal** smoldering in it. Place in the **Cauldron** a mixture of:
   Ginger   Wormwood   Anise Seed   Balm of Gilead
   Cubeb Berries   Red Sandlewood

4. Place these times in a **White Bag**:
   Scarab   Asafoetida   Ash Leaves   Mulberry Leaves
   Moon seed (or Tillia Star)   Your Hair

5. Anoint **Bag** with **Starry Wisdom Oil**. Put bag on **Altar**, light **Candles** and hold the **Athame** with both hands, blade pointed downward into the **Cauldron**. While **Incense** smolders stir the smoke counterclockwise and say:

This is my world,
you have no place in my world
you cannot enter my world
This is my world
nothing can touch me
nothing can harm me
nothing evil may exist in my world.

When you have concentrated, and said the chant 9 times, snuff out candles and place a bag over the door or in your pocket.

Repeat the ritual the next 9 nights or until candles have completely burned out.

To Make Troublesome People Leave You Alone

1. Take a **Black Cloth Doll** in a **Waning Moon** and stuff it with dirt from the person's property (if not attainable, write the person's name on **Parchment Paper** in **Ritual Black Ink**).

2. Place the Paper along with:
   Dillweed   Devil Shoe String   Elecampane
   Cowslip   Elderberries
   into the doll. Sew it shut. Tie the hands and feet together with **Black & Red String** and place on cloth on the altar between a **Red & Black Candle** anointed with **Bind & Drive Oil**. Sprinkle Doll with **Get Away Powder** and say:

   > His/Her hands and feet I wind
   > Their interference to bind,
   > they may not harass me
   > as I myself stay free
   > they deeper and deeper entangle
   > themselves in their mangle
   > no more to bother me
   > Then, I set them free

3. Burn **Drive & Bind Incense** during ritual. Blow out **Candles** and put **Candles, Dolls, Cloth** and **Ashes** from **Incense** in a box and hide in a dark place. When person stops bothering you, you can cut the threads that bind them and throw it all into running water.

To Discover the Identity of an Enemy

1. On a **Monday** or in a **Moon Hour,** take a **Gold** or **Orange Candle** and anoint with **Mercury Oil.** Burn **Mercury** and **Papyrus Incense** together in your Thurible. Scratch on the **Candle** *"Who Has Done This?"*

2. Draw this figure on your **Altar** in Chalk: Place **Candle** in circle part of the figure and say:

> Brothers of other evolution's
> seek and find
> who has done these abomination
> Reveal to my mind
> make them be revealed to me
> what they have done
> so I may be free
> and success can come

The identity of your enemy will be revealed in a dream or a meditation.

Protect Your Relationship from interference

1. On a **Saturday** in a **Waxing Moon,** a few nights before a **Full Moon** in a **Venus Hour,** prepare your Altar with these items:
   a. **White Cloth**   b. **Old Shoe that belongs to your Mate**
   c. **Old Piece of your White Clothing that has been worn but not washed**
   d. **White Image Candle representing your Mate**
   e. **Has No Hanna Oil**
   f. **Freya/Frey Oil**   g. **Freya/Frey Incense**
   (If you are a male doing this spell on a mate use Frey
   If you are a female doing this spell on a mate use Freya)

2. Mix these herbs together:

Devils Shoe String	Deer's Tongue	Honeysuckle
8 Morning Glory Seeds	Angelica	Blessed Salt
Five Finger Grass	Blue Stone Powder	

Altar
N

```
      1
      2
E     2      W
  4       5
      6
```
S

1. Image Candle
2. Bowl
3. Salt
4. Herbs
5. Incense
6. Shoe

3. Place the **Piece of clothing** on the **Altar** and anoint the **Image Candle** with **Oils.** Place the **Candle** in a bowl (preferably white) with **Herbs** and **Blue Stone.**

4. Put your **Mate's Shoe** in the front of the **Candle** and sprinkle **Blessed Salt** in a circle clockwise around the bowl with the **Image Candle** and the **Shoe.**

5. The **Incense Burner** with **Incense** smoldering should be on the right hand side of the Altar. Light the **Image Candle** and place both hands on either side of the **Image** and say:

> Goddess Freya/God Frey, protect my mate
> from others admiring glances
> from others jealousy and hate
> Protect him/her from flirtations
> keep our relationship strong
> protect our bonds and relations
> keep us together, loyal and long

6. Concentrate for a few minutes on your love and snuff out the **Candle**. Do the chant and burn the **Candle** until the day/night after the **Full Moon**. Then let the **Candle** burn itself out on that day.

7. Put the **Wax** and **Herbs** from the bowl into your **Mate's Shoe**. Wrap the **Shoe** in your clothing and hide somewhere safe from prying eyes. This will keep your relationship safe from unwanted interference.

Protect Your Mate in Travel

Make the following Mojo Bag(s) on a New Moon Night Hour

1. AIR TRAVEL:
   If your mate is traveling by air used a **White Mojo Bag** and anoint it with **Air Oil** and **Protection Oil**. After anointing the **Mojo Bag** place the following items in it:

Eye of the Cat	Swallows Heart	Cassia Buds
Coriander Seed	Cardamon	Rosemary
Blue Lace Agate Stone		

   Close the Bag and hold it between your hands for a few moments, then tie the **Mojo Bag** closed 3 times. (Close all bags in same manner)

2. WATER TRAVEL
   If your mate is traveling by water use a **Blue Mojo Bag** and anoint it with **Water Oil** and **Protection Oil**. After anointing the **Mojo Bag** place the following items in it:

Cats Eye Shell	Irish Moss	Moon Stone
Peppermint	Kelp	Sea Salt

   Close the Bag and hold it between your hands for a few moments, then tie the **Mojo Bag** closed 3 times.

3. GROUND TRAVEL
   If your mate is traveling by ground use a **Green Mojo Bag** and anoint it with **Earth Oil** and **Protection Oil**. After anointing the **Mojo Bag** place the following items in it:

Eye of the Cat	Black Cat Bone	5 Fingergrass
Sage	Sandlewood	
High John the Conqueror		

   Close the Bag and hold it between your hands for a few moments, then tie the **Mojo Bag** closed 3 times.

4. **A**LL **P**URPOSE

   If your mate is traveling by all 3 use a **Red Mojo Bag** and anoint it with **Elemental Oil** and **Protection Oil**. After anointing the **Mojo Bag** place the following items in it:

   Beth Root   **Sage**   **Jalap**
   Rosemary   **Agate Stone**
   Close the Bag and hold it between your hands for a few moments, then tie the **Mojo Bag** closed 3 times.

Place the **Mojos** in the appropriate places if your Mate will not carry them on their persons:

Travel by Air or Water - in a Suitcase

Travel by Ground - in a Car

If your Mate is not receptive to the **Mojo Bags** at all, you may sew the Bags in the lining of the suitcase or hide in the car or burn the mojo Bags and sprinkle the ashes in the suitcase or car. If you still have a non-receptive Mate, boil the **Mojo Bags** one at a time and sprinkle their belongings with the water. Do not carry the boiled Mojo Bags, bury them.

ourt Spell - Innocent

To be protected and come out successful in a court situation.

If you are **not guilty** of a situation and wish to have a **favorable verdict** in court, start this spell on a **Waxing Moon** on a **Jupiter Day (Thursday)**.

1. Get a **Brown Male Image Candle** and anoint it with **Just Judge Oil**. Burn the **Candle** in a bowl of **Brown Sugar**. While burning **Jupiter Incense** concentrate on a favorable outcome and a fair verdict. Say:

   > Judge be just
   > I win without a care
   > Victory a must

2. Burn the **Candle** a few minutes a night, while doing your chant, until the **Candle** has melted completely.

3. Take the **Wax** that has melted and mix it with the **Brown Sugar**. Throw it near the **Court House** in some **Bushes** or **Shrubs**. If there is no foliage about the **Court House**, take the items in a **Brown Paper Bag** and throw it away in a **trash receptacle** in the Court House. Continue burning the **Jupiter Incense** until you must go to court.

 Court Spell - Guilty

If you are guilty and wish a lesser sentence.

If you have committed a crime and are now repentant and want to receive a less harsh penalty.

1. Anoint a **Red & Brown Combination Candle** with **Court Oil**. Scratch your first **petition** into the **Wax** of the **Candle** or on a piece of **Parchment Paper** in **Dragon's Blood Ink** to be placed underneath the Candle Holder. Make certain you state in your petition that you are sorry and will not do "this thing again. This is very important!

2. Burn **Wolf's Heart Incense** while burning the **Candle** and place on the **Altar** a **Red Bag** containing:

   1 John the Conqueror Root   1 Galangal Root
   1 Beth Root   1 tsp Ginger
   1 Wishbone

3. Anoint the **Red Bag** with **Courage Oil** and leave on the altar during the spell. Burn the **Candle** and the **Incense** each night for 15 to 20 minutes concentrating on your wish for protection from the law and the state and say:

   My Life is real
   The crime is repented
   I have now relented
   My life will change
   for the better I know
   My future I rearrange
   into a straight and smooth flow

4 When the **Candle** is completed, (it may take 7 nights or more) bury the wax far away from your home. Carry the **Bag** and keep it anointed with **Courage Oil** until the court situation is completed to your favor then burn the bag.

   Spell will not work or will revert if you are not truly repentant!

P rotect Yourself from Ill Health

Make this doll on a New Moon in a Sun Hour.

1. Make or buy a **Blue Magic Doll** representing yourself and stuff it with:

   A few **Hairs from your head**   **A Seal of Rabcaleb**
   A Healing Heart   **1 Tsp each of these Herbs:**
   Lavender, Rosemary
   Lemon Verbena
   Thyme, Hyssop, All Heal

2. Sew the **Doll** shut with **White Thread** and anoint once a week on a **Wednesday Evening.** Keep the **Doll** safe in a **Cedar Box** lined with **Life Everlasting Flowers.** The **Doll** will protect you from ill health for one year.

3. Then the **Doll** and **Life Everlasting Flowers** must be placed in a **Bag of Blessed Salt** and released into a **River, a Stream** or the **Ocean.**

4. A new **Doll** needs to be made and placed in the **Box** with **New Life Everlasting Flowers** to keep the protection current.

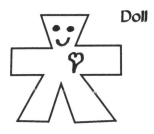

Doll

Protection Yourself from injury

Perform this spell on a Mars Day in a Mars Hour,

1. Take 5 Whole Licorice Roots and tie them together with Red Yarn to form a 5-Pointed Star.

2. In the center of the Star, hang a small Red Bag containing the following items:

   Master of the Woods (Woodruff)
   Mistletoe
   Mugwort
   Magnolia Leaves
   Mustard Seeds (yellow)

Star

3. While your are making the Star and the bag, burn a Red & Purple Combination Candle anointed with Tetragramation Oil and burn Tetragramation Incense. When the Star and the Bag are completed, pass both through the rising Incense smoke and say:

   Earth, air, fire, spirit and water
   protect me from injury and bother
   Tetragramation be my defender
   protect me from all and every offender

4. Hang the Star in your home and burn Tetragramation Incense once a week.

   This spell needs to be done twice a year. Once when the Sun is in the sign of Aries and next when the Sun is in the sign of Scorpio. The Star that has lost it's effectiveness and should be disposed of after the new one is made.

Protect Relationship from anger and Resentment

1. Each **Month**, just after the **Full Moon**, sprinkle **Rue Herb** and **Poke Root** around your home. Sweep out the front door and into the street or vacuum up the herbs and throw away out the front door.

2. Hang an **Orange Bag** filled with **Passion Flowers** and **Sacred Bark (Cascara Sagrada)** over your front door. Be sure to anoint it once a month with **Selket Oil.**

   If an argument between you and your mate does occur, sprinkle Purslane Extract around the room to cool angry tempers.

Safflower Spell for Court

For protection from someone giving evidence against you in court.

1. On a **Sunday** in a **Sun Hour**, anoint a **Scarab** with **Myrrh Oil** and put the **Scarab** in a **Leather Bag** filled with **Safflower Petals** and place it on your altar.

2. Burn **2 Yellow Candles** on either side of the bag containing the **Scarab** and say:

> May nothing rise up against me in evidence
> May no hindrance be against me
> May no enemy give testimony against me
> May my name hold no evil against me
> May no lies be uttered in my presence
> Behold I am exonerated
> Behold I am acquitted
> Behold all charges against me are dropped
> Behold I am innocent of all charges
> Behold I am free and able to go my way

3. Carry the **Scarab** and **Safflower Petals** around your neck or in your pocket from now on and keep it anointed with **Myrrh Oil** each week.

Protection from Slander

*Start spell on a Waxing Moon on a Jupiter Day
and a Jupiter Hour.*

1. Fill a small **Red Bag** with **Slippery Elm Bark** and place a **Sharks Tooth** in the Bag.

2. Anoint the **Bag** with **Athena Oil** and **Athena Incense** while the candles are burning and say:

> May lies turn into flies in your mouth
> by the flaming sword of the truth from south
> may maggots be your daily meal
> if Athena, your lips can not seal
> If you cannot say something nice
> may your teeth be splintered twice
> but, if you are kind to me
> blessed you shall be

3. Do the spell each night over the bag until the candles are burnt down. Then wear or carry the bag and keep it anointed once a week.

To Remove a Personal and/or Family Curse

If you feel you or your family has been cursed for a day or for generations, perhaps by an old Voodoo or Gypsy type curse.

1. Take a Black Skull Candle anointed with Spell Breaking Oil *(if skull is not available, use Image or Cat Black Candle)*. Burn for **8 nights**, starting at the **Full Moon**. Burn for 15 minutes a night while you concentrate on the evil being burnt away.

2. On the **8th night**, in the crevice of the **Skull** made by the burning wax, place these Herbs:

   Agrimony   Dill   Rue
   Five Finger Grass (or Lucky Hand)
   St. Johnswort   Wormwod

3. On top of the **Herbs** place a **Seal of Mephistopheles** and Seal **All**, the **Herbs** and the **Seal** with the drippings from a **White Candle**. When the **Herbs** are a tightly sealed in the **Skull Candle** put the **Candle** in a Gray Bag or some Gray Material and sprinkle with **Graveyard Dust** and **Goofer Dust**. Take it to a graveyard and bury it.

That particular type of spell will be broken forever and no new spell of evil of that type can be placed upon you or your family ever again.

Hex Away a Trouble

1. Make this **Hex Sign** on **Parchment Paper** in **Dragon's Blood Ink** with a **Black Quill Pen:**

Diagram.....  Write your trouble in great detail on the back of the seal.

2. Light a **Black Candle** that has been anointed with **Banishing Oil** and place the **Parchment Paper** in front of it with the seal face down.

3. Take **1 tsp.** of **Lobelia** and **1 tsp.** of **Boldo Leaves** and place them in the middle of the back of the seal where your petition is written.

4, Roll up the **Herbs** in the seal, rolling the seal away from you and towards the **Candle.**

5. Seal the rolled **Parchment Paper** with a few drops of **Black Wax.** Take the **Candles** remanents and the **Seal** far away from home and bury them.

To bring good luck to your life, anoint a Wish Bone with New Life Oil and hang over your bed.

P rotect Yourself from Violent

Spell should be done on a New Moon Night

1. Take a **White Bag** and place in it a **Lucky Hand Root** and fill it with **Five Finger Grass, Blessed Salt** and **Jimson Weed.** The bag will be worked with for the next 3 nights.

2. Light **2 White Candles** anointed with **Banishing Oil** and burn **Banishing Incense.** Hold the **White** prepared **Bag** in your hands and as you are breathing the words onto the Bag and say:

> I Banish from me all feeling of fear
> I am safe when this amulet is near
> evil people that wish me harm
> will not find any undo alarm
> for I appear confidence and self assured
> there are easier victims to be lured

4 On the third night let the **Candles** burn completely down and bury the **remnant** and sprinkle the ground with **Blessed Salt.** Then carry the bag with you at all times and no harm shall come to you.

To Drive Someone Away from Your Mate

This spell may be one of the most important ones you ever use to drive away the negative influences of mate's friend(s). It can be used to remove the influences of an unwanted admirer(s) of your mate who could potentially steal them away or destroy your relationship with your chosen mate.

Begin this spell in a Moon Hour on a Monday in a Waning Moon or just after a Full Moon is optimum.

Materials:

Black to White Candle *(black on top and white on bottom)*
Parchment Paper   **Dragon's Blood Ink**   **Drive & Bind Oil**
Drive & Bind Incense   **Devil's Bit (Scabious)**

Write these symbols down on a square piece of **Parchment Paper** in **Dragon's Blood Ink**.

```
S D P N QC N
D P N QC N
P N QC N
N QC N
QC N
C N
N
```

1. Write the Person's name on the back of the seal that you wish to be driven away. Place a small amount of **Devil's Bit** in the center of the **Seal** and burn to ashes with the **Drive & Bind Incense**.

2. Anoint the **Candle** with **Drive & Bind Oil** and burn the Candle while concentrating on the purpose to be accomplished. When you have concentrated for as long as you can - about 15-20 minutes - blow out the **Candle** and take the **Ashes** from the burnt **Seal** and the **Incense Ashes** and sprinkle on your steps or front door.

3. In the morning, sweep them away or into the street. Repeat the spell, making the **Seal**, burning the **Incense**, **Candle**, etc. do this until the **Candle** is completely burnt, by then the person who is bothering your mate should have gone.